TRUSTING GOD

TRUSTING GOD

A LIFE WITHOUT WORRY

Margaret Feinberg

Foreword by Sheila Walsh

THOMAS NELSON
Since 1798

NASHVILLE   DALLAS   MEXICO CITY   RIO DE JANEIRO

© 2012 Thomas Nelson

All rights reserved. No portion of this book may be reproduced, stored in a retrieval system, or transmitted in any form or by any means—electronic, mechanical, photocopy, recording, or any other—except for brief quotation in printed reviews, without the prior permission of the publisher.

Published in Nashville, Tennessee, by Thomas Nelson. Thomas Nelson is a trademark of Thomas Nelson, Inc.

Thomas Nelson, Inc., titles may be purchased in bulk for educational, business, fund-raising, or sales promotional use. For information, please e-mail SpecialMarkets@ThomasNelson.com.

Unless otherwise noted, all Scripture quotations are taken from THE NEW KING JAMES VERSION. ©1982 by Thomas Nelson, Inc. Used by permission. All rights reserved.

Scripture quotations marked NIV are taken from HOLY BIBLE: NEW INTERNATIONAL VERSION®. ©1973, 1978, 1984 by International Bible Society. Used by permission of Zondervan Publishing House. All rights reserved.

ISBN: 978-1-4185-4929-9

Printed in China

11 12 13 14 RRD 5 4 3 2 1

Contents

Contents

Foreword

Trust is an interesting word. It's one of those small words, like *love*, that weighs a lot and really packs a punch. I remember seeing the movie *The Jungle Book* when I was a little girl and being horrified by Kaa, the snake who could hypnotize anyone who stared into his eyes long enough. His compelling line to Mowgli, the boy hero in this Rudyard Kipling tale, was "Trust me!" According to my mother, I yelled out for all to hear, "Don't do it Mowgli!" Trust is costly if the one you place it in is not trustworthy.

I think most of us would agree that as we grow and learn, we understand that trust has to be earned. I remember once being on a blind date that had been set up by friends of mine. The guy seemed nice enough at first, but when he asked me if I was open to having children, before we were even through with our main course, I decided that he had no concept of the appropriateness of building trust!

When we talk about the commitment to trust God, most of us would say that we do trust him, probably admitting that we'd love to trust him more. Of all the issues we talk about as Women of Faith, trust seems to be the most foundational. Over the last few years this issue of trusting God had been very much on my heart and in my prayers. I want to trust Him 100 percent with everything I have and everything I am, but at times I have struggled to do that. Whenever I struggle with any area of my faith, I turn to God's Word. The psalmist David said it so beautifully,

Your word is a lamp to my feet and a light to my path.
Psalm 119:105 (ESV)

As I began to study God's Word more in depth and to look at the lives of many of those that Margaret will introduce us to here, one thing became clear. It's not that the men and women we will meet in this study overcame fear on their own and became superheroes of the faith; it's that they gained a greater understanding of who our awesome God is.

I believe that is the key to trusting God and living a life without fear. When we understand that our God is on the throne and nothing can happen to us today or tomorrow that hasn't passed through his merciful, loving hands, then we begin the awesome adventure of trusting him with abandon. It's so clear to me now that it's not about us; it's all about God.

Take a man like Job. In Job 1:1 we read that he "was blameless and upright, one who feared God and turned away from evil." He was a good man who served God with a full, obedient heart, yet God allowed the enemy to decimate his life. What I find most compelling about Job's story is this. Beyond the heartache and the loss, the pain and suffering, we have this profound statement from Job at the end of his story:

My ears had heard of you before, but now my eyes have seen you.
Job 42:5

I find that amazing! He was regarded as the godliest man on the earth at that time, yet it took God pulling back the curtain just a little and showing himself to Job to change everything. In Job's experience he went from knowing about God in his head to seeing Him, and that changed everything.

That is my prayer for you. As Margaret leads us through this study, may you see our Father, may you behold his son Jesus, and because of who he is, may you never be the same again.

—SHEILA WALSH

Introduction

God's Invitation to You

*Worry is like a rocking chair; it'll give you
something to do, but it won't get you anywhere.*

UNKNOWN

Worry and stress have a way a sneaking into our lives when we're not looking. God invites us to wave goodbye to this unwelcome duo and learn to depend on him in everything. As worry and stress disappear in our rearview mirror, we discover new things about God, life, and others that we never imagined.

Throughout this study, we will look at men and women who faced challenging situations and impossible odds but discovered the power of relying on God every step of the way. Whether it's Noah leading a herd of wild and whimsical creatures on a wooden boat, Abraham leaving everything familiar to venture into the great unknown, or Ruth embarking on an unforgettable love story, we're reminded that the same God who led, guided, and protected them, leads, guides, and protects us too. Their journeys are powerful reminders that no matter what we are facing, we can trust God.

My prayer is that throughout this study, you will find yourself growing in the faith and trusting that God has everything under control—even the smallest details of your life. I hope that in response you will bravely say yes to everything God is calling you to do.

Blessings,

Margaret Feinberg

God Is
in the Details

*When it comes to relying on God, we find comfort in
knowing that God is with us. But that kind of **with** isn't
a distant and far off kind of presence; no, God is **with**
us in the minutest details of our lives. Whatever we're
facing, God has a way of surprising us with his presence
and reminding us that nothing escapes his notice.*

One

Noah's Big Boat Adventure

Noah was a brave man to sail in a
wooden boat with two termites.

UNKNOWN

Noah didn't have a single reason to worry—he had hundreds of furry and scaly reasons. God selected this unsuspecting man for an unusual task: he was asked to go into the boat-building business.

Noah didn't know the first thing about seafaring, so the request must have caught him by surprise. Build a boat. Fill it with animals. Prepare for rain. However, through his obedience, Noah would save himself, his family, and a boatload of animals from a worldwide flood.

Why did God select Noah? We don't know all the reasons, but Genesis tells us that God regretted He had made humankind (Gen. 6:6). In fact, God actually grieved and felt sadness in His heart. However, when God looked across the earth, He noticed one man who was different: Noah. This blameless and righteous man not only walked with God but found great favor with God. So God approached him with some good news and some bad news. God chose to deliver the bad news first. Everything on the earth was going to be destroyed. But the good news was that Noah and his family were to be saved. All they had to do was build a boat and climb aboard. Sounds crazy, right?

When Noah and his family finally stepped on dry ground again, Noah had only one response: to worship God.

The Bible tells us Noah did everything God asked of him—which was no small feat. God was specific about not only the dimensions of the boat but also the kind of wood Noah should use. When he finished the boat, Noah gathered the animals, just as instructed, and he and his family climbed aboard. They waited. Noah's neighbors must have thought he was crazy.

When the first raindrops hit the wooden deck, Noah and his family knew he wasn't crazy after all. Noah had obeyed God and responded with faith. As the waters rose, worry probably set in. How long would the storm last? Would the boat hold together? Had he packed enough food for all the animals? For his family? Yet Noah discovered that the same God who had instructed him to build the ark was still leading and guiding and providing as they all waited for the waters to subside. When Noah and his family finally stepped on dry ground again, Noah had only one response: to worship God.

Through Noah's life, we're reminded that faith challenges us to push aside our worries and our stress and trust God no matter how unusual the circumstances. Though we may face unexpected situations, we can choose to live by faith. We can be people like Noah who are righteous and who walk with God.

1. Read *Genesis 6:5–8*. How was Noah different from the other people on the earth?

2. What do you think differentiates the righteous from the unrighteous? Make a list of characteristics for each in the space below.

Characteristics of the Righteous	Characteristics of the Unrighteous

3. *Which of the characteristics listed above best describe you? Are there any changes in your attitude or actions that you need to make to become more righteous?*

4. *Read* **Genesis 6:9–21.** *What emotions do you think Noah felt when he heard God's instructions (Gen. 6:13–21)? What worries and doubts do you think Noah experienced as he built the ark? Make a list below.*

5. *Reflecting on your list of the emotions, worries, and doubts Noah experienced, which ones do you tend to wrestle with in your own life?*

6. Read **Genesis 8:14–21.** What was Noah's priority once he emptied the ark (**Hint: Gen. 8:20**)? What does this reveal about Noah's relationship with God? What does it teach us about our own priorities?

7. What does the story of Noah's adventure aboard the ark reveal to you about the nature of God?

8. How are you challenged and encouraged by Noah's story to trust God more in your own life right now?

Sometimes God sets us on an unexpected course in which we are asked to trust Him with every detail of the journey. God is worthy to be trusted and worshipped as we respond in obedience.

Digging Deeper

Hebrews 11 is often referred to as the Hall of Faith—where a handful of characters from Scripture are commended for their great faith and trust in God. Read **Hebrews 11:1–7.** Who are the first three people commended in the listing of faith heroes? What do they all have in common? What do you think are some of the greatest qualities of Noah that you want to emulate in your own life?

Bonus Activity

Use a search engine like BibleGateway.com to find other places where Noah is mentioned in Scripture (*Hint: Matt. 24:36–44 and 2 Peter 2:4–6*). What insights do you gain about Noah and about God as you reflect on these passages?

Two

Isaac's Unforgettable Love Story

Trust the past to God's mercy, the present to
God's love, and the future to God's providence.

AUGUSTINE OF HIPPO,
CHRISTIAN THEOLOGIAN

One of the greatest love stories of all time is tucked into the book of Genesis and displayed in the unlikely meeting of Isaac and Rebekah. So many circumstances had to align perfectly for these two individuals to come together. What if just one *what-if* didn't work out?

Abraham had fallen in love with Sarah, his wife of many years, and longed for his own son Isaac to experience the same kind of loving and intimate relationship. Abraham also knew that if the promises God had given were to come true—namely, that he would be the father of many nations—Isaac needed a baby. But before a baby, he needed a bride. What if he fell in love with a foreign woman who did not share his love for the one true God? What if he found no one suitable back home with his old clan? With all the pressures, Abraham was tempted to worry.

Abraham wasn't the only one who felt the pressure. Instead of sending his own son to search for a bride, Abraham turned to his trusted servant to find the perfect wife for Isaac. Abraham asked the servant to find a wife who was not a Canaanite but was instead one of his own relatives. Think of the poor servant and the endless refrain that ran through his mind as he crossed every dusty mile: *What if the woman won't come back with me to this land?* (Gen. 24:5, 39) The what-ifs flooded his mind.

God has absolute control over everything, all the details of life—even the circumstances that led to the marriage of Rebekah and Isaac.

Even after the servant identified a very special woman, Rebekah, at the well, the what-ifs didn't end. What if Rebekah was tired and didn't want to water a stranger's camels? What if her father refused to allow Rebekah to her leave her native land? Those familiar with the story know that all the what-ifs worked out because a powerful, sovereign God was in control all along. The word *sovereign* means that God has absolute control over everything, all the details of life—even the circumstances that led to the marriage of Rebekah and Isaac.

We all face a barrage of what-ifs every day. If left unchecked, they can wreak havoc with our hearts, minds, and emotions. What if I end up alone? What if my rebellious child never learns to harness his actions? What if the doctor says it's serious? But there are greater what-if questions we can ask ourselves. What if we choose to trust God with all the details? What if we choose to pray? What if we choose to walk in faith? What if we choose to follow God's instructions fully and faithfully?

What if the same sovereign God who brought Isaac and Rebekah together is still sovereign over our lives today? What if God has something better than we ever expected waiting for us around the next corner?

1. *Take turns reading* **Genesis 24:1–9.** *What was the servant's immediate what-if question regarding the oath his master asked him to take* (**Hint: Gen. 24:1–5**)? *When in the past week have you responded to a situation or person with an immediate what-if question?*

2. *Read* **Genesis 24:10–14.** *When in the last week have you asked the Lord for something specific as the servant did? What was the response?*

3. *Stressful situations are always less stressful when we turn to the Lord in prayer instead of turning inward with worry. How often do you turn to the Father when you are facing what-ifs? Place an "x" along the continuum below. What prevents you from turning to the Lord more frequently?*

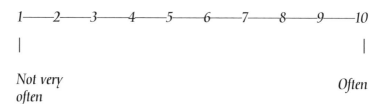

1———2———3———4———5———6———7———8———9———10

| |

Not very   *Often*
often

4. *What are three great what-ifs you are facing in your life right now?*

5. *How are you handling each of the three what-ifs you listed emotionally? Spiritually?*

6. *Use the space below to write out a personal prayer to the Lord about the what-ifs you listed in question four. Be specific in your request so you will recognize how and when God answers.*

Many times throughout Scripture, God is described as being sovereign, meaning He has absolute authority over everything. The story of the extraordinary meeting of Isaac and Rebekah displays a beautiful facet of God's sovereignty—the knowledge that we can find God at work even in the smallest details.

7. *Take turns reading **Genesis 24:15–67**. What does the story of Isaac and Rebekah reveal about the sovereignty of God? When in your life have you seen evidence of God's sovereignty?*

8. Which what-if questions in your life do you need to surrender to God knowing that everything is under His control and nothing escapes His notice? Which what-if questions have been holding you back from growing in trust and walking in obedience to God?

> What-ifs cause worry and stress. As children of God, we can walk in obedience and trust, knowing that God has all the details under control.

Digging Deeper

Read **Luke 22:39–46.** How did Jesus respond to the big what-if before His arrest? What is the biggest what-if question you have ever faced? How did you respond? What can you do now in your daily spiritual walk that will prepare you for the big what-if moments in life?

Bonus Activity

Spend some time researching other men and women in the Bible, such as Jonah, Mary, Moses, Peter, and Thomas. Make a list of the what-if questions they faced. Compare and contrast the what-if questions in their lives to those in your own.

Three

Hagar Is Pursued by God

*One day we will meet beside the river and our
Lord will dry every tear. For now, we must live in
the joy of that promise and recall that for every
generation life is hard, but God is faithful.*

BODIE THOENE,
AUTHOR

Hagar wasn't just Sarah's maid; she helped run the household. Whenever Sarah needed something, Hagar was quick to respond, ready to serve. One day Sarah approached Hagar with an unexpected request—would Hagar bear Abram a son since Sarah was barren?

Hagar agreed and probably believed she was honoring Abram and Sarah. But after the conception of her son, Ishmael, everything changed. Tensions at home began to rise. Sarah's attitude toward Hagar was cold, her tone harsh, and her demands unfair. Hagar tried to do what was right, but everything seemed to be going wrong.

Layered with worry and stress, Hagar felt as if she had no choice. She fled. She knew deep down that running away wouldn't solve anything, but what else could she do? She found a spring in the desert and sat alone in her misery. Hot sun beating down; tears probably streaming down her face. She had no way out. Hagar had done everything she knew to do. No one on earth understood the pain and isolation she felt. But God did. In the hot, dry, dusty desert, Hagar learned one of the greatest lessons any human can ever learn—God sees us. We are never alone.

In the hot, dry, dusty desert, Hagar learned one of the greatest lessons any human can ever learn—God sees us. We are never alone.

God met Hagar in her lowest moment. When she was at her wits' end, running away from problems that were too big for her to bear, God met her in a profound way. But the truth is that God had been by her side through it all. In an incredible desert meeting with God, Hagar didn't experience the slightest judgment or condemnation for the way she was feeling. Instead, the Lord met her with compassion and a promise for a better tomorrow.

There is little doubt that the encounter with God in the desert stuck with Hagar for the rest of her life. In that place, Hagar met God and gave Him a very personal name: The God Who Sees Me.

Isn't it comforting to know that when no one seems to notice the heavy burden you bear or the stress and worry you feel inside, there is a God who sees you too? He will meet you in moments of misery and speak words of promise to you just as He did for Hagar. Lift up your eyes; see the One who sees you.

1. Read **Genesis 16:1–6**. If you asked both Sarah and Hagar to give their perspectives on what happened in this passage, they would probably tell wildly different stories. Why is it important to always hear the other side of the story?

Overwhelmed by her overbearing and cruel mistress, Hagar fled into the wilderness. She had nowhere to turn and no one who seemed to be on her side.

2. When was the last time you felt hopeless, as Hagar did? What restored your hope?

Hagar didn't just continue wallowing in her sorrows—someone met her in her time of greatest need.

3. Read **Genesis 16:7–16.** *Place a check mark by each statement that you imagine Hagar wished the angel had said to her. Then circle the promise the angel actually gave to Hagar in the desert.*

____ *Sarah would be nicer to her now.*

____ *Hagar would have a son.*

____ *Circumstances at home would improve.*

____ *Abram would defend Hagar.*

____ *Hagar would have too many descendants to count.*

4. *When was the last time you found yourself in a situation like Hagar's, where the instruction or encouragement you received from the Lord wasn't exactly what you wanted to hear? How did you respond?*

Years later, Hagar ended up in the desert again. This time she was sent away by Sarah rather than running on her own.

5. Read *Genesis 21:8–21*. What are the similarities and differences between the two trips to the desert?

6. What do both journeys reveal about the faithfulness of God?

7. What comfort from Hagar's encounters with the Lord do you find in your own life right now?

8. *Look up each of the passages in the table below. In the second column, write down the promise each verse makes. Which of these passages gives you the most hope for your life right now?*

Scripture	Promise
John 1:12	Example: Whoever believes in Jesus will not stay in darkness.
Proverbs 22:9	
Psalm 46:1	
Isaiah 43:1	
John 11:25	
Isaiah 54:10	

Even when no one on earth understands the impossible situation you're facing, God sees you. That's a powerful encouragement to not worry but instead trust in the God who sees.

Digging Deeper

The book of Jeremiah was written thousands of years ago to a people living in exile. Read **Jeremiah 29:11.** What promise does God give to His people in this passage? What encouragement does this passage bring you right now? How do you think Hagar would have responded if she had read this passage in the desert?

Bonus Activity

Take a survey among your friends or fellow church members to see what their favorite promise of God is. Write down all the promises in one place and keep them in your journal or Bible. Bring them out and read them for encouragement the next time you experience a middle-of-the-desert moment as Hagar did.

Four

Sarah's Echoing Laughter

All will be well, and all will be well, and
all manner of things will be well.

JULIAN OF NORWICH,
CHRISTIAN MYSTIC AND THEOLOGIAN

As the wife of Abraham, Sarah spent years hoping, praying, and yearning for a baby. Sarah may have even eaten a few unusual foods that well-meaning friends suggested would help her become pregnant. When you really want a baby, you will do nearly anything to make your dream come true.

Sarah grew old waiting for a child. Though so much was at stake—her family's future, the promises of God, her own reputation—Sarah finally came to terms with the fact that she would never have children. She was barren. Somewhere along the way she allowed herself to stop being a lady who hadn't had children *yet* to a disgraced and disappointed old woman who couldn't give her husband a son. The one thing she had hoped for all those years was never going to happen. All hope was gone as far as she was concerned.

But as far as God was concerned—and He always had been concerned about his daughter, Sarah—the impossible for her was more than possible for Him. God had a master plan, not only for her life but also for the life of her unborn son and an entire nation. The Lord sent messengers to speak to Sarah's husband, Abraham, about the barrenness. These men showed up out of nowhere and promised she'd become pregnant. When they suggested something so absurd, Sarah couldn't help herself; she literally burst out with laughter. Becoming pregnant at her age was silliness.

As far as God was concerned, the impossible for her was more than possible for Him.

For God, however, this was no laughing matter! An aged body was no barrier for a God who specializes in the miraculous. God didn't need any help or manipulation from Sarah. All He needed was room to be God. Sarah needed to surrender her hopes and disappointments and lost dreams to the One who had the power to change her broken, barren heart into a fertile breeding ground of faith.

In some ways Sarah's story is every woman's story. We all have hopes and dreams in our hearts. Some come true with relative ease. Others require hard work on our part. Yet others are impossible for humankind, but somehow by the grace of God our hopes and dreams are fulfilled when we least expect them and in ways we never imagined.

Regardless of whether our desires land in the *fulfilled* or *not yet* category, we can always be certain that God sees and understands our hearts. It may be that He chooses to wait to fulfill our hope, or it may be that God will turn our sorrow into laughter just as He did for Sarah.

1. *Read* **Genesis 18:1–16.** *How did Abraham's and Sarah's responses differ toward the three visitors and the news they brought? How do you think you would have responded to the news?*

Abraham and Sarah received the news that they were going to be parents after decades of barrenness. The Lord remained faithful to Sarah and Abraham, but Sarah displayed a lack of faith and laughed at the ridiculous news of a promised son.

2. *In the last three months, when have you found yourself laughing at impossible situation as Sarah did? How was your laughter received?*

25

3. In Genesis 18:14, God asked Abraham a rhetorical question. How does this question challenge you in your own life right now?

Sarah believed her problem of barrenness was too big for the Lord to handle. Instead of trusting God, she took the situation into her own hands. As we learned in chapter three, Sarah (her name was Sarai before the Lord changed it to Sarah) decided to find another heir for Abraham.

4. Reread **Genesis 16:1–5**, or think back to what you learned in chapter three. What was the result of Sarah's (Sarai's) taking matters into her own hands?

5. When in the past month have you taken matters into your own hands rather than trusting God? What was the result?

God didn't just leave Abraham and Sarah with the promise of a prospective son; He kept his promise.

6. Read *Genesis 21:1–7*. How did God remain faithful to Sarah and Abraham? What was Sarah's response?

7. When in the last year have you seen God's faithfulness specifically on display in your life or someone else's life?

8. What hopes and dreams have you been hesitant to surrender to God? List three of them here, and ask God to fulfill the desires of your heart according to His will.

Even when it seems all hope is gone, we can still choose to trust God. Nothing is too hard for the Lord.

Digging Deeper

The gospel of Luke describes the lives of two cousins who long to have children. Read **Luke 1:5–38.** Compare and contrast the responses of Zechariah, Elizabeth, and Mary to the news of an upcoming birth. How do their stories display the truth that "For with God nothing will be impossible" (v. 37)?

Bonus Activity

Do you know anyone who is struggling with infertility? Women often suffer in silence and feel hopeless and frustrated after years of trying to conceive. Stop and say a prayer for any friend or relative who comes to mind. Ask the Lord to be gracious to her just as He was with Sarah and Elizabeth.

God Is in the Big Picture

God isn't just with us in the details; He is also in the big picture. God doesn't just go with us; he goes before us preparing the way. Though sometimes we encounter mind-bending challenges and crazy circumstances, the Alpha and Omega, the beginning and the end, still has it all under control. So there's no need to worry.

Five

Joseph's Unexpected Rise to Power

*To accomplish great things, we must not only act,
but also dream; not only plan, but also believe.*

ANATOLE FRANCE,
FRENCH POET

As a young man, Joseph was a dreamer. Then Potiphar's wife found him too dreamy to resist. Next thing he knew, he was interpreting the dreams of others. And eventually, through countless twists and turns and a few nightmares, Joseph's own long-ago-dreamed dreams came true.

You can't help but wonder if Joseph's story would have turned out differently if he had just kept his dreams to himself. Without the dreams, his brothers wouldn't have been tempted to throw him in a well (at least not that day!). And if Joseph hadn't been thrown in a well, he wouldn't have been sold at the perfect time to a traveling caravan and wouldn't have ended up in the service of Potiphar. And without Potiphar, Potiphar's wife (who later accused him of impropriety) wouldn't have tempted Joseph. And without the false accusation, Joseph wouldn't have ended up in prison where he eventually interpreted a few dreams.

Without those dream interpretations, his name wouldn't have been brought to the king and Joseph would never have been named number two in power over all of Egypt.

Without the dreams that God put in his heart as a young man, Joseph's story could have been wildly different.

Without the wise Joseph being in charge of saving supplies during the seven years of provision in preparation for the seven years of famine, all the people of the land would have died during the lean years. It is hard to imagine what or where Joseph would be without his dreams!

Without the dreams that God put in his heart as a young man, Joseph's story could have been wildly different. God gave Joseph those dreams, and He did so for a reason. The whole Israelite nation avoided certain death in the famine because of those dreams. In fact, when you get right down to it, history was altered because of those dreams.

Joseph received God-given dreams. He was destined for greatness. He was created for a purpose. Joseph was called by God and set apart for His service with important Kingdom work to do. That did not mean everything was easy for Joseph. Not at all. It did mean, however, that no matter what stressful situation Joseph faced, the Almighty God was in charge of his destiny. God was at work behind the scenes, regardless of the worry and fear and dark, lonely times in more than one pit.

Isn't that good news for us today? Sometimes God allows situations that challenge and stretch us. At times we may be tempted to worry, but all along the way, God invites us to trust Him and call on His name.

1. Take turns reading **Genesis 37:1–11**. How did Jacob's treatment of Joseph stir up sibling rivalry?

2. When have you experienced or expressed parental favoritism? What was the result?

3. What were the specific dreams God gave Joseph that made his brothers so angry they wanted to kill him? When in the last month have you had jealousy stir inside of you, just as Joseph's brothers did? How did you respond?

Joseph's brothers became so jealous and angry they sold Joseph to Ishmaelite slave traders and faked his death. The traders then sold Joseph to Potiphar—an officer to the king of Egypt and the captain of the palace guard. The Lord was with Joseph, and Joseph was put in charge of Potiphar's household. While Potiphar trusted Joseph with everything, Potiphar's wife had plans that broke that trust.

4. Read *Genesis 39:1–20.* How did Joseph respond to the temptation presented by Potiphar's wife? How have you been tempted in the last month? How did you respond to the temptation?

Because of Potiphar's wife's deception, Joseph found himself in prison. The Lord remained with Joseph throughout the temptation and his trials.

5. In all the places and lands that Joseph traveled and lived, the Lord was with him. Match the place or predicament on the left with the Scripture that tells of the Lord's presence on the right. Describe a time when you have felt God's presence in your life no matter what the circumstance.

Place or Predicament	Scripture
In prison	Genesis 39:23
In Potiphar's house	Genesis 39:20–21
In whatever he did	Genesis 39:1–6

The Lord remained faithful to Joseph even when he was in prison, and Joseph was put in charge of other prisoners. Joseph deciphered two dreams for fellow inmates. One man, Pharaoh's cupbearer, shared Joseph's gift of dream interpreting with Pharaoh. Yet Joseph knew very well from whom came his blessings and any power he had.

6. *Read the following verses below and match them with the correct passages in the right column. When in the last week have you given credit to the Lord?*

Scripture	Joseph Credits God
Genesis 40:8	"It is not in me; God will give Pharaoh an answer of peace."
Genesis 41:16	"Peace be with you. Do not be afraid. Your God and the God of your father has given you treasure in your sacks; I had your money."
Genesis 43:23	"But now, do not therefore be grieved or angry with yourselves because you sold me here; for God sent me before you to preserve life."
Genesis 45:5	"Do not interpretations belong to God? Tell them to me, please."

Joseph used his God-given talent of interpreting dreams to tell Pharaoh what his dream meant. Pharaoh noticed the Lord's presence with Joseph and rewarded him for his actions. Joseph had gone from the pit to the palace, back to a pit, and was now second to the king.

7. When have you seen God use unusual circumstances to bring you to the place He wanted you to be?

8. Despite the temptations and trials we face, it's comforting to know that God is always by our side. What dreams have you given up on or let go of that God wants you to trust Him with?

God can be trusted with all your dreams—big or small. He has a plan and a purpose for your life. Even when the stresses of everyday life come, He is there working behind the scenes on your behalf.

Digging Deeper

Read Ephesians 3:20–21. What comfort do you find in knowing that you serve an immeasurable God? When are you tempted not to trust the Lord with your relationships? Job? Family? How can you be more intentional about trusting the Lord to be in control of everything?

Bonus Activity

Do you know someone who has given up on her dreams of happiness or purpose? Write a hand-written note of encouragement to her about what you have learned through Joseph. You may be just the positive encouragement she needs to keep the faith.

Six

Esther's Divine Moment

*All I have seen teaches me to trust the
Creator for all I have not seen.*

RALPH WALDO EMERSON,
AMERICAN PHILOSOPHER AND POET

During the feast of Ahasuerus, on the seventh day, King Ahasuerus
called for his wife, Queen Vashti, but she refused to obey. The
king responded by dethroning her. After the queen was removed, a
kingdom-wide search for a new queen began. Among the candidates
was a young Jewish woman named Esther, who was looked after by
her foster father and biological uncle, Mordecai. Despite the unlikely
odds, Esther won a nationwide beauty pageant and was crowned the
new queen.

What sounds like the beginning of a fairytale actually happened.
The book of Esther records this amazing story.

Through a series of unforeseen circumstances, Mordecai saved
the king's life. Mordecai's sudden rise to fame and good fortune
infuriated one of the king's men, Haman, who developed a plan to
kill not just Mordecai, but all of the Jews. Neither Haman nor the

king realized that Queen Esther herself was a Jew and therefore condemned under the new law.

Esther found herself in a very precarious position. The weight of the world was on her shoulders. Would she choose to obey God and stand courageous in the midst of incredibly difficult circumstances? Or would she buckle under the pressure? In the end, Esther chose to surrender to the Lord and used her newfound favor at an opportune moment to uncover the plot and save the Jewish people. When Haman's evil plans were discovered, Haman was hanged on the gallows he had built for Mordecai.

Esther was willing to put her worries aside and act in faith, saving her own life as well as the lives of thousands of others.

Though stress and worry could have gotten the best of Esther, preventing her from saving God's chosen people, she overcame her fears. She placed her trust in God and exclaimed, "If I perish, I perish!" She was willing to put her worries aside and act in faith, saving her own life as well as the lives of thousands of others.

One of the most interesting details about the book of Esther is that throughout its pages you will never find God mentioned. Not once! But God was still at work. Esther's story reminds us of divine providence in every aspect of our life, even when we're not aware of it. Even when we are not aware of His presence, God is still with us, orchestrating a story and an ending that is beyond anything we can imagine.

1. *The book of Esther is full of larger-than-life Bible characters who played a role in the story of a beautiful young Jewish girl saving God's people. Using what you learned in the introduction story, along with the Scripture listed on the left, match the character*

with his or her role on the right. Who is your favorite Bible character? Why?

Scripture	Character
Esther 4:11–5:2	Esther
Esther 1:11–12	Vashti
Esther 2:21–23	Mordecai
Esther 1:19	King Ahasuerus
Esther 3:56	Haman

Role
Saved the king's life
Approached the king without being summoned
Banished his wife for not obeying and chose a new one
Refused to approach the king when summoned
Hated Mordecai and all the Jews

The characters in Esther make up an interesting cast in the story of how one woman's bravery and courage saved her people. When Mordecai learned of Haman's plot, he charged Esther with an important, but life-threatening, duty.

2. Read *Esther 3–4. Esther had reason to worry and stress. What were the consequences for the Jewish people if she attempted to help them and failed? Describe a time in your life when something big depended on you. How did you handle the situation?*

3. According to Esther 4:11, what could have happened to Esther when she approached her husband, the king, without being summoned to him?

4. How willing would you be right now to obey God if he asked you to do something that might cost you your life or the lives of others? Mark an "x" along the continuum for your answer. What factors would make you more willing or less willing to take a huge risk?

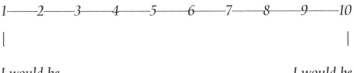

1———2———3———4———5———6———7———8———9———10

| |

I would be   I would be
very unwilling   very willing

5. When have you found yourself in a position "for such a time as this," as Esther did, where you were uniquely at the perfect place to serve God or help others (**Hint: Est. 4:14**)? How did you respond to the situation?

Because of Esther's willingness to risk her life in order to save her people, King Ahasuerus did not destroy the Jews and rewarded Esther for her boldness.

6. Read *Esther 7*. What evidence of the providence of God do you see in this chapter?

7. Though God is never actually mentioned in the book of Esther, His work is seen throughout. In what ways do you recognize the unseen hand of God working behind the scenes in Esther's story? In your own story?

8. Where in your own life is the Lord asking you to take a step of faith right now?

> *We don't have to worry, because God is at work even when we don't recognize it. We can trust God with everything.*

Digging Deeper

A portion of Paul's letter to the church in Rome unpacks the principle of God working on our behalf. Read **Romans 8:28.** How did all things work together for Esther's good? What examples do you see of God taking a bad situation and bringing good from it in the story of Esther? What does this mean for your own life?

Bonus Activity

Listen to the Crystal Lewis song "For Such a Time as This." Close your eyes and listen to the words. How does this song encourage and challenge you in your own journey of faith right now?

Seven

Moses Protests His Divine Calling

Where God guides, he provides.

Unknown

The story of Moses contains unexpected twists and turns. As an infant, Moses was given up by his natural mother and placed in a basket in a river, but then he was rescued by the daughter of Pharaoh only be raised by his natural mother after all. Moses grew up in a palace and received the best training available in all of Egypt. That was just the beginning of his crazy life. Moses grew up as a prince in a huge palace but found his heart was still with his true people—the Israelites.

Maybe that's why on an average day, while Moses was caring for the flocks of his father-in-law, God revealed himself to Moses in the form of a bush that was on fire but would not burn up. Holy. Pure. Unexpected. God asked Moses to go to Pharaoh and secure the Israelites' freedom. Moses' blood pressure skyrocketed. He could feel the anxiety, the angst, and the apprehension settling in. *Why should I go to Pharaoh? Who am I to do these things?* Moses wondered. A laundry list of concerns echoed through his mind: *What if they don't believe me? What if they don't listen? Doesn't God know I'm not a good public speaker? No one will understand me!*

The story of Moses reminds us that while we encounter doubt and worry in life, nothing God calls us to do is greater than His ability to provide.

Moses' feelings of inadequacy threatened to overtake him. He felt completely incapable and unprepared for what God was asking him to do. But one by one, God addressed his concerns. The Lord provided help in the form of Moses' brother Aaron. He spoke words of encouragement and assurance to Moses. After a litany of excuses, Moses finally agreed, and because he obeyed, the entire Jewish nation was freed from slavery in Egypt. To this day, Moses is seen as a picture of Christ. Just as Moses delivered Israel from the slavery of Egypt, Jesus Christ delivered humanity from the slavery of sin.

The story of Moses reminds us that while we encounter doubt and worry in life, nothing God calls us to do is greater than His ability to provide. Though we may be tempted to feel anxious or angst-ridden, we are invited to turn to God and ask Him to meet our needs through prayer. Any excuse we have for not obeying God is something that can be overcome with God's strength. We don't have to fall to pieces or live in a basket-case state of worry. All we have to do is be open and honest before the Lord, and God will help us move forward in obedience despite our feelings of inadequacy.

1. Read **Exodus 1–5** and **Exodus 12–13** for a review of the highlights of Moses' journey. Place the following events in chronological order. What was your favorite part of Moses' story?

___ Moses was placed in a basket in a river.

___ Moses offered every excuse in the book, but God provided a way to obey in every instance.

___ Pharaoh let God's people go free.

___ Moses saw the burning bush while tending the flocks of his father-in-law.

___ After a series of plagues, God instructed Moses and Aaron to observe the first Passover.

___ Moses lived in the palace with his adopted Egyptian princess mother

___ Moses went to Pharaoh and asked for freedom for all the Jews.

2. Review Exodus 3-4. During Moses' encounter with the burning bush, he felt overwhelmed with inadequacy. When in your own life have you been overwhelmed by feelings of inadequacy? How did you respond?

3. *What was Moses' response when he heard God call to him from within the burning bush (**Hint: Exodus 3:1–6**)? How do you respond when you feel God asking you to do something?*

4. *When God called Moses, he responded with a laundry list of concerns and reasons why he wasn't the best candidate. Look up the following passages. What are Moses' concerns? How does God address each one?*

Scripture	Moses's Concern	God's Response
Exodus 3:11–12	Who am I that I should go?	
Exodus 3:13–14	What if they ask me, "What is His name?"	
Exodus 4:1–9	What if they do not believe me?	
Exodus 4:10–12	O Lord, I have never been eloquent.	
Exodus 4:13–16	Please send someone else to do it.	

5. *What are some of the most common excuses or reasons you provide when it comes to avoiding what God asks of you?*

6. *How do you find that God responds to the excuses or reasons for disobedience that you provide Him?*

7. *What is an area in your own life where the Lord is calling you to do something but you feel inadequate or afraid to obey?*

8. Which lessons from Moses' life are sources of encouragement for the challenges you face in your own spiritual journey right now?

At times you may feel inadequate to do the very things God has created and called you to do, but you can find confidence knowing that the God who has chosen you will be with you every step of the way.

Digging Deeper

Like Noah, Moses is also mentioned in Hebrews 11 as part of the Hall of Faith. Read **Hebrews 11:24–28.** What facets of Moses' life and character are celebrated in this passage? If you were you to include your name and story in Hebrews 11, what would you want said about yourself?

Bonus Activity

Create an acrostic with the word *faithful*, having each letter begin an encouraging word about who God is and why you can trust Him.

Eight

David Dances with Wild Abandon

The great thing, and the only thing,
is to adore and praise God.

THOMAS MERTON,
WRITER

David was an extraordinary man. Not only was he a shepherd and a king, but he was a poet, a songwriter, and a musician. Described as a "man after God's own heart," David loved to worship God. While his words and music line the pages of the book of Psalms and are quoted throughout the New Testament, one of the most striking portraits of David's worship appears shortly after the Ark of the Covenant (where the Ten Commandments were held) is brought into Jerusalem.

David had gathered 30,000 men to travel to Baalah to retrieve the ark. When they arrived, they decided the best way to transport the ark was to place it on a new cart. As the cart rolled toward Jerusalem, tens of thousands of Israelites worshipped and celebrated with great passion.

Then something went awry. One of the oxen stumbled. Uzzah, walking alongside the ark, reached out to make sure the ark didn't fall to the ground, though it was against God's law for anyone to touch it. Uzzah died instantly from God's anger. What seemed like an innocent act was actually an expression of irreverence.

If ever there was reason for King David to celebrate, it was the presence of the Almighty God in the city.

David was both angered by and fearful of the incident. Instead of delivering the ark to Jerusalem, he decided to take it to the house of Obed-Edom the Gittite. For three solid months, Obed-Edom and everyone in his household was wildly blessed. That's when David realized he had made a mistake. David returned to the home of Obed-Edom to gather the ark and bring it to Jerusalem. Along the way, he worshipped with abandon.

David couldn't contain himself and danced before the Lord with all his might. He leaped. He twirled. He whirled. One can only imagine the delight and joy that emanated from him as he expressed his adoration.

Stress level: zero.

Worry list: nonexistent.

David did not care a bit what people thought of him or whether neighborhood tongues wagged. The ark of the Lord was entering the city, symbolizing God's great presence among His people. If ever there was reason for King David to celebrate, it was the presence of the Almighty God in the city.

This image of David dancing with reckless abandon stands in stark contrast to Michal, David's wife, who watched David's dancing from the window. Rather than join in the delight, the levity, the beauty of the moment, she despised David in her heart (2 Sam. 6:18).

Undoubtedly, worry and uneasiness had gotten the best of Michal. She was worried about what people were going to think of their king acting in such an undignified manner. Rather than seize the moment in joy, she pushed it–and David–away. She missed her moment.

You can't help but wonder how Michal's response might have been different if she had chosen to re-center her heart on celebrating the presence of God. What if she had gone down into the street and joined her husband in worshipping the Lord? What if, instead of thinking about what others might say, she had concentrated on what *God* would think of the extravagant display of worship? She could have traded all the angst, stress, and concern she was feeling for a once-in-a-lifetime chance to be part of something special.

The story of David and Michal demonstrates how important it is to concentrate on God alone. It's a reminder that we should take the worry and stress of trying to please others and trade it for a simple desire to please God. Instead of worrying, we can choose to worship.

1. David worshipped the Lord through music and by dancing. What is your favorite form of worship? Why?

2. Read *2 Samuel 6:1–15*. Which of the following activities was David engaged in as part of his worship before the Lord? Place an "x" next to each activity.

____ Rejoicing

____ Blessing others in the name of the Lord

____ Singing "In Christ Alone"

____ Sacrificing burnt offerings

____ Shouting

____ Playing his harp

____ Waving a banner

____ Listening to trumpets blasting

____ Leaping

____ Holding hands with his wife

____ Dancing before the Lord

____ Celebrating before the Lord

3. Of the activities listed above, place a check mark next to those responses that are most natural for you to use as expressions of worship. Now place a circle next to those that are the most difficult for you to use as an expression of worship. What is the difference for you between the two?

4. When have you been in such awe of God that you found yourself spontaneously worshipping him? Write about your experience below.

5. Read **2 Samuel 6:16**. Why do you think Michal was so worried and concerned about David's worship?

6. How concerned are you typically about how others view you or what they think of your actions? Place an "x" along the continuum to mark your response.

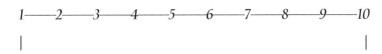

1———2———3———4———5———6———7———8———9———10

| |

I am very concerned   *I am not concerned*
about how others   *about how others*
view me.   *view me.*

7. 2 Samuel 6:16 is one of the last details the Bible records about the life of Michal. Based on this passage, would you describe her life as marked by hope or by heartbreak? Explain.

8. When David was dancing and praising God with all his might, he didn't have any space or energy for worrying about anything else. What can you do to foster a greater sense of abandon in your worship of the Lord?

When we choose to worship rather than worry, all our anxiety and concerns melt away in the presence of God. Worship is always the better choice.

Digging Deeper

God selected David, an unlikely candidate, to become king over Israel. Read **1 Samuel 16:3–13.** According to this passage, what is the Lord looking for in a leader? When you choose to focus on the Lord instead of worrying about what others may think, what changes do you notice in yourself? How can you sharpen your focus when distractions threaten to pull your attention away from God?

Bonus Activity

Grab your iPod or CD player and put on one of your favorite worship songs which is most meaningful to you. Let the words and music penetrate your heart, and try your hand at dancing with all your might before the Lord. (You may want to find a space to be alone for this activity!)

God Is in the Everyday

*God isn't just in the details or the big picture;
He's also in our every day. God is with us in the
ordinary nine to five and five to nine revealing
Himself and His love for us. God steadily reminds
us throughout the Scriptures that there is no reason
to worry; we simply need to turn to Him.*

Nine

Cain's Reminder About What Is Truly Important

*I know the power obedience has of making
things easy which seem impossible.*

TERESA OF AVILA,
NUN AND THEOLOGIAN

Cain and Abel both brought offerings to the Lord. One, the gift
of the field; the other, the gift of the flock. While Cain's gift of the
field was rejected, Abel's gift of the flock was accepted. Why? The
Scripture doesn't specifically say, but something was incomplete or
missing from Cain's offering. Maybe it was a token offering rather
than the firstlings given by Abel. Whatever the reason, Cain didn't
just become angry; he became *very* angry. His countenance fell.
Dangerous emotions surged.

The Lord approached Cain with some reassuring words, "If you
do well, will you not be accepted?" Then God warned Cain that if he
didn't do well, sin was waiting to get the best of him. What a moment!
Cain was invited by the very Creator of the universe to stop worrying

about Abel and simply trust Him. All Cain had to do was give his best offering and everything would turn around. No more nervous tension. No more competition. No more bitterness toward his brother. Destructive emotions of hurt, jealousy, anger, and outrage would be replaced with relief, peace, love, and joy.

God was waiting for Cain to release all the emotional worry to Him and focus on the important stuff. Cain made the wrong choice.

But Cain refused. He killed his brother. He lost sight of everything that was truly important. Cain had a choice. He could have trusted God, accepted the Lord's correction, and walked in obedience; or he could let sin get the best of him and ruin his life (not to mention cutting his brother's life short). Emotions were racing, jealousy surging in his bones. Anger was threatening to choke out all reason. God still offered him a way out; God was waiting for Cain to release all the emotional worry to Him and focus on the important stuff. Cain made the wrong choice.

Like Cain, we have a choice to make when worry, anger, and jealousy rise within us. We can stop and listen to the calm, reasoning voice of God, or we can choose to take matters into our own hands. Only through our relationship with God can our destructive thoughts and feelings be transformed and redeemed into constructive expressions that bring life and hope.

1. Read Genesis 4:1–16. Make a list of the emotions Cain may have felt in this passage. Then circle the emotions you've experienced in your own life.

_____   _____

_____   _____

_____   _____

2. Cain centered his negative emotional response on Abel. When you find yourself in situations where you're upset, who are the three people you most often direct your emotional responses toward?

3. As in Cain's story, have you ever encountered a situation where you wished you had done the right thing and obeyed God? What happened?

4. When negative and harmful thoughts swirl in your mind, what spiritual and everyday practices are the most helpful for calming your stress? Circle the techniques you've tried before and place a star by the ones that work best for you.

___ Bubble Bath

___ Write in Journal

___ Go for a Walk

___ Grab the Ben & Jerry's

___ Call a Friend

___ Pray

___ Read the Scripture

___ Light Candles

___ Punch a Pillow

___ Watch TV/Movie

___ Talk to a Christian Mentor

___ Other

_____

_____

In many of his letters, Paul begins in the indicative mood (giving facts and posing questions) and then shifts to the imperative mood (expressing a request or a command). For the book of Romans, chapter 12 is where Paul makes the shift from the indicative mood to the imperative—he calls the church in Rome to be set apart from the world.

5. *Read* **Romans 12:1–2.** *In the last three months, when have you found yourself responding to a situation in which you were conforming to the world?*

6. *In the last three months, when have you found yourself responding to a situation in which you were being transformed by the renewing your mind? What made the difference between conforming and being transformed?*

7. Read **Philippians** 4:8. In the table below, make a list of the eight things on which Paul instructs believers to focus. Then record a statement from your own life that demonstrates that focus.

Paul Instructs Believers to Focus On	How My Life Demonstrates That Focus
Example: True	God has given me the opportunity to demonstrate his love to others today.

8. Take a few quiet moments before you close. Make a list of three to five people in your life who stir up harmful emotions as Abel did for Cain. Write just the first initial of their first names in the space below. Then write down three things about each person that you appreciate. Spend a few moments in prayer for each person on your list. How did your attitude and emotions change as you blessed and prayed for each individual?

> *When swirling emotions threaten to take over, we have a choice. Let's choose to obey God, surrender all our anxiety, and let peace reign in our hearts and lives.*

Digging Deeper

No matter what emotional or physical storm we're confronted with, God can calm the waters of our soul and spirit if we turn to Him and obey. Read **Psalm 107:29** and **Mark 4:39.** When in your life has the still voice of the Lord calmed you? What was the effect of the Lord's presence in your life? Emotions? Circumstance? Take some time to listen for the still voice of God right now.

Bonus Activity

Try something you rarely make time to do . . . relax! Draw a warm bath. Light some candles. Put on your favorite praise music. Crawl in and exhale. Spend the next 20 minutes pouring out all your emotions in prayer to the God who cares so much about you. Ask God to help you refocus on how you can live an obedient life before Him.

Ten

Abraham's Big Decision

There is no other method of living piously and
justly, than that of depending upon God.

JOHN CALVIN,
THEOLOGIAN

Originally known as Abram, though we'll call him Abraham for
ease of reference, he was called out of Ur into the adventure of a
lifetime following God. However, despite the very clear and powerful calling of God, it wasn't long before Abraham began to question
God's provision and promises. He allowed the worries of what *could*
happen interfere with his trust in God to take care of him and his
family.

When famine swept the land, Abraham headed to Egypt. Rather
than turn to God, he let worry and stress get the best of him. Abraham convinced his wife, Sarah, to lie and play the part of his sister
because he was afraid that Pharaoh and the Egyptians would have
him killed in order to steal her from him. When Pharaoh discovered
the deception, he spared the couple's lives, but forced them to leave
the land.

Fast forward out of Egypt and into a new land. Yet again Abraham is placed in a challenging situation.

Abraham left behind a legacy of extraordinary faith and trust even though he made mistakes.

As Abraham and Sarah settled into the region of Gerar, Abraham again lied to a king. Out of fear, he told Abimelech, the king of Gerar, that Sarah was his sister—not his wife. Abimelech took Sarah, thinking she was unmarried. The Lord confronted the king in a dream telling him Sarah was Abraham's wife. Abimelech returned Sarah to Abraham and sent them on their way.

Abraham was not perfect. His deceptions were definitely not a reflection of someone who wholeheartedly trusted in God. However, he learned from his mistakes and slowly learned to make better choices and to trust God through his mistakes. When he was later given the ultimate test of faith and asked to sacrifice his own son, Isaac, Abraham passed with flying colors. In fact, Abraham went on to become one of the heroes of faith referred to throughout the Old and New Testaments. When you hear the great stories of Abraham's faith, there is rarely any mention of the two parallel incidents of his not trusting God and instead taking matters into his own hands. Rather, we hear of his rock-star status as "God's friend" and his rock-solid faith that still inspires today.

Abraham left behind a legacy of extraordinary faith and trust even though he made mistakes. We can follow Abraham's example when we make the mistake of letting stress and worry get the best of us. We can learn from whatever mistakes we have made and decide to trust God instead. We can choose to walk in obedience *now*, regardless of past errors in judgment. The best is yet to come.

1. What does it mean to you personally to serve the God of Abraham?

2. When was a time you took matters into your own hands and chose deception over honesty? What was the result?

On two separate occasions, Abraham made the same mistake. He told two different kings that Sarah was actually his sister, not his wife. Instead of choosing what was honest, he chose deception. Thankfully, the Lord intervened on his behalf to make things right.

*3. Read **Genesis 12:10–20**. How did God intervene despite Abraham's mistake?*

4. Read *Genesis 20:1–18*. How did God intervene despite Abraham's mistake? When have you seen the Lord intervene on your behalf despite your mistakes?

5. What similarities and differences do you see in these two stories about Abraham deceiving the leaders? Write the differences in the outer circles and the similarities in the overlapping inner circle.

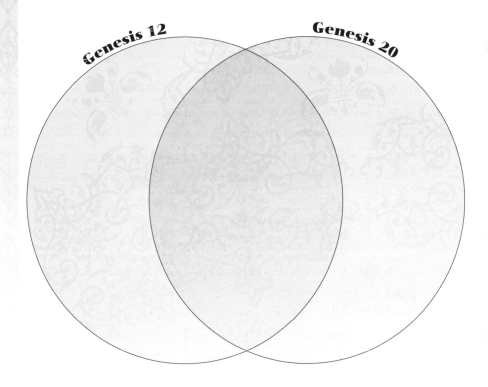

Genesis 12   Genesis 20

Abraham yet again struggled with trusting the Lord and told the king that Sarah was his sister. This was a reoccurring temptation in Abraham's life, yet the Lord still chose to use Abraham to be the father of many nations.

6. Have you ever made a huge mistake and not trusted God when you should have? What did you learn from the experience?

We often make big mistakes when we choose to do things our way, as Abraham did. While our past may seem to taint our future, God chooses to forgive and forget our mistakes. He is so much bigger than our past, and He wants to do something bigger with and through us despite our mistakes.

7. Do you feel defined by your past mistakes? Mark your answer on the continuum below. What is blocking you from feeling fully free and forgiven?

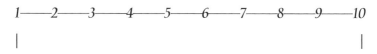

1——2——3——4——5——6——7——8——9——10

I feel defined
and trapped by
my past mistakes.

I feel freed from
and forgiven for
my past mistakes.

The Lord offers hope and freedom from our past mistakes. He still chooses to forgive us and use us despite anything we have done.

> *8. How can you more fully trust the Lord in everything despite mistakes you have made?*

Worrying about past mistakes only robs us of future progress. God will still forgive, teach, and use us for His glory. Even when we fail Him, He never fails us.

Digging Deeper

Despite his many mistakes, Abraham is still known for his faith. Read **Romans 4.** What is credited as righteousness toward Abraham (v. 3)? Verse 13 makes a significant point in Paul's argument. Fill in the blanks of verse 13: "For the _____ that he would be the heir of the world was not to Abraham or to his seed through the _____, but through the righteousness of _____." In light of what you know about Abraham's past mistakes, how are you encouraged by Abraham's faith after reading this passage?

Bonus Activity

Choose two to three members of the Hall of Faith in Hebrews 11. Read their stories in the Old Testament. List out at least one mistake each person made and learned from before they became the giant of faith they are known as today.

Eleven

Ruth's Amazing Rescue

The faithful person lives constantly with God.

CLEMENT OF ALEXANDRIA,
CHRISTIAN THEOLOGIAN

The book of Ruth follows the adventures of Ruth, a young Moabite woman whose life is marked by loss and heartbreak. Her husband suddenly died, and so did his brother, leaving Ruth and her sister-in-law behind. Meanwhile her mother-in-law, Naomi, was also a widow. The women were left with nothing. They had no way to provide for themselves and no husbands to protect and care for them. During this time in history, living as a single woman was unheard of and unsafe. The women were in a very precarious situation. Food was scarce and they could not provide for their modest home.

Unsure of what to do or where to turn, Naomi wanted to travel back to her homeland far away in search of food and a new beginning. Ruth's sister-in-law stayed behind, but Ruth went with her mother-in-law to the land she left so long ago. All Ruth knew of this place was through the stories and tales she had been told. In her desire to start over, Ruth adopted the God of her mother-in-law, the one true God, as her own Master and Lord. She placed all her trust in Him and left everything that was familiar, striking out for a new life in a new land. No doubt the young widow worried about her uncertain future with each step on the long road.

Naomi didn't direct Ruth to Boaz's field or she wouldn't have asked Ruth where she worked that day after she came home.

The pair arrived in Bethlehem at the beginning of the wheat harvest. When they arrived, Naomi sent Ruth to the fields to gather grain from the edges of the fields, as was the custom for orphans and widows in that day. Ruth obeyed Naomi and worked her fingers to the bone out in the field. The owner of the field, Boaz (who happened to be a wealthy kinsman of Naomi's husband), took notice of the hard-working, beautiful young woman. He started asking around to find out more about her. Her reputation for being a loving, loyal, kind person reached his ears and penetrated his heart.

Ruth found more than food in Boaz's fields during that harvest season. She found true love. Boaz eventually decided to redeem Ruth by marrying her. Through this amazing series of circumstances, Ruth became the grandmother of King David and one of only four women listed in the genealogy of Jesus, the Messiah. Ruth's story reminds us that though we're tempted by worry and stress, God works through all kinds of circumstances and situations for His glory.

1. Read Ruth 1. How would you describe the relationship between Ruth and Naomi? Who in your life has been a Naomi to you?

2. Read **Ruth 2.** *When in your life have you had to humble yourself and allow someone else to take care of you? What did you learn about yourself and God from the experience?*

Naomi instructed Ruth to glean the fields of her relative Boaz. Gleaning was an instruction given by God.

3. Read **Leviticus19:9–10.** *Ruth engaged in the practice of gleaning, or gathering crops that would otherwise be left in the fields. What are some practical ways you leave the corners of your field untouched so that others can benefit?*

4. Read **Ruth 3**. *Much of the story of Ruth and Boaz's relationship is based on redemption. God had set laws in place to protect widows and family inheritances. What do the following passages reveal about the religious laws concerning widows?*

Leviticus 25:23–28:

Deuteronomy 25:5–6:

The book of Ruth demonstrates the power of God to transform a life from hopelessness and sorrow to hopefulness and joy. Naomi chose to put her hope in God and found God working through the unexpected love story of Ruth and Boaz to provide for her. However, the story doesn't end there.

5. Read **Ruth 4:13–22**. *According to this passage, who is Boaz and Ruth's great-grandson? What does this genealogy reveal about the connection between Ruth and Jesus Christ (**Hint: Matthew 1:1–17**). What does the genealogy reveal about the faithfulness of God?*

6. *In the last three months, what specific situations or circumstances in your life (or someone else's life) have tempted you to believe they were beyond God's redemption or restoration?*

7. *Throughout the story of Ruth, God provided for the physical and spiritual needs of Ruth and Naomi. How do you see God at work in your life meeting specific physical and spiritual needs?*

8. *What specific needs are you facing right now that sway you toward worry and stress rather than trust and faith? Spend some time in prayer asking God to meet every need.*

Though we are faced with seasons of loss and pain, God has a plan to not only provide for us but also heal us. We simply need to turn and trust Him.

Digging Deeper

Read 1 Peter 1:18–19. What did Jesus have to do in order to become a kinsman redeemer for us? What parallels do you see between Boaz as Ruth's kinsman redeemer and Jesus as our kinsman redeemer? In what areas of your life do you still need to make God your refuge and redeemer?

Bonus Activity

Spend some time reflecting on all that God has given you. What are some corners of your field from which you could allow others to benefit? Consider donating extra food from your pantry, extra clothes from your closet, or extra tools from your garage to those in need.

Twelve

Elijah's Divine Visitation

We can do all things with the grace of God,
which he never refuses to them who ask it
earnestly. Knock, persevere in knocking, and
I answer for it that he will open to you.

BROTHER LAWRENCE,
MONK

Elijah had a lot to be worried about! The queen had placed a bounty on his head and Elijah had nowhere left to turn. He had just experienced one of the coolest, most in-your-face "God" experiences in the entire Old Testament when God defeated the prophets of the false god Baal on Mount Carmel. One minute, Elijah is on top of the world; the next, he's running for his life. The queen was ultrapowerful, after all. And she loved those false prophets that Elijah had slain. Now Elijah had a target on his back, as Queen Jezebel had all the resources of the kingdom focused on catching him and ending his life.

The faithful prophet decided to give up, throw in the towel, call it kaput. He ran for his life into the wilderness, sat down under a tree, and begged God to take his life. Literally, the stress and worry drove Elijah over the edge. He couldn't take it anymore. The constant pursuit of his powerful enemy had caught up to him. Elijah just wanted to check out of life altogether. He begged God to just make it all stop.

Elijah's story reminds us that wherever we are and whatever we're doing, God can draw near.

But God refused to let go of Elijah. An angel appeared to Elijah and delivered bread for him to eat and water to drink. The sustenance miraculously gave Elijah the strength to hike all the way to Mount Horeb, known as the mountain of God, a place where other leaders had had profound encounters with the Lord.

When Elijah arrived at Mount Horeb, he found a cave and crawled inside. Elijah wasn't just trying to hide from the evil Queen Jezebel; he was also trying to hide from the rest of the world. But God met him there. After all, the Lord makes sure His children are never truly alone. A sudden wind whistled through the sky. An earthquake shook the ground. A fire descended from heaven. Elijah remained safely tucked inside the cave until he heard a gentle whisper. That's when Elijah could no longer resist the tug on his heart. He walked to the cave's entrance and had a profound encounter with God in which God assured him that all his concerns were not only heard but also met. His worries fled; the stress melted away. Elijah was reenergized for the long road ahead.

Elijah's story reminds us that wherever we are and whatever we're doing, God can draw near. Just a few words from God can change everything.

1. Read **1 Kings 18:1–19:2.** What caused Elijah to run for his life?

2. When was the last time you tried to flee from a situation as Elijah did? What was the result of running away?

3. When was the last time you faced a situation that left you feeling discouraged, depressed, or despondent? What and who helped get you out of the slump?

4. As Elijah sat under the tree in the desert, he probably experienced a long list of concerns. Reflecting on Elijah's story, rank the following list of worries in order from greatest to least concerning. Which would have been your number one concern if you were Elijah? Why?

___ Elijah was worried that Jezebel and Ahab would continue to rule the land.

___ Elijah was worried that he would not have food to eat or water to drink in the desert.

___ Elijah was worried that he was the only one who still faithfully followed God.

___ Elijah was worried that God didn't notice or care for him.

___ Elijah was worried that his life and ministry were over forever.

5. When in the past year have you felt emotionally, physically, or spiritually overwhelmed by stress and worry? How did you handle the situation?

6. When was the last time you heard the still voice of God in your life? What was the result of your encounter with God's voice?

7. Look up the following verses. How does God respond to each of Elijah's worries and concerns?

Scripture	Elijah's Worry	God's Response
1 Kings 19:16	Elijah was worried that Jezebel and Ahab would continue to rule the land.	
1 Kings 19:5–6	Elijah was worried that he would not have food to eat or water to drink in the desert.	
1 Kings 19:18	Elijah was worried that he was the only one who still faithfully followed God.	
1 Kings 19:11	Elijah was worried that God didn't notice or care for him.	
1 Kings 19:15	Elijah was worried that his life and ministry were over forever.	

8. How does God's response to Elijah in 1 Kings 19 encourage you in your own faith journey right now?

Even when we are emotionally, spiritually, and physically overwhelmed by stress and worry, God longs to speak to our souls in a gentle whisper and assure us of His presence and purpose for our lives.

Digging Deeper

Read **1 Kings 19:19–21** and **Luke 9:57–62.** What do these passages reveal about what wholehearted obedience and commitment to God looks like? Are there any areas of your life in which you are tempted to offer only partial obedience or commitment to God?

Bonus Activity

If you are able, take a few hours to go outside and take a hike or brisk walk in the fresh air. Look for a tree and sit under it for a while. Think of Elijah as he sat under the tree in the desert, completely overwhelmed. Pour your heart out before the Lord and watch how He ministers to you and strengthens you for your journey ahead.

Leader's Guide

Chapter 1: Noah's Big Boat Adventure

Focus: *Sometimes God puts us on an unexpected course in which we're asked to trust Him with every detail of the journey. God is worthy to be trusted and worshipped as we respond in obedience.*

1. *Noah found favor and was righteous. Noah was blameless in his time and walked with God.*

2. *Answers*

Characteristics of the Righteous	Characteristics of the Unrighteous
Holy	Angry
Pure	Bitter
Kind	Unforgiving
Gracious	Jealous
Generous	Envious
Peaceful	Gossipy
Patient	Backbiting
Loving	Malicious
Forgiving	Hateful

3. *Answers will vary, but often we display characteristics of both righteousness and unrighteousness in our lives. God calls us to live righteously.*

4. *This question is designed to help participants imagine what it was like to be Noah and feel the fear, excitement, thrill, joy, angst, stress, self-doubt, and passion Noah felt when he obeyed God.*

5. Participants may resonate with several, if not all, of the emotions, worries, and doubts that Noah experienced.

6. During this hectic and uncertain time, Noah chose to worship and honor God—a wonderful lesson and reminder to all of us of what's truly important.

7. The story reveals that God is holy. God is just, and sin will not go unpunished. God demonstrates His mercy and grace by sparing some. God demonstrates His power through the flood. God shows His attention to detail throughout the particulars of the story, including which and how many animals are placed on the ark.

8. Just as Noah trusted God before, during, and after the flood, we can be challenged to trust God in all circumstances.

Digging Deeper

Abel, Enoch, and Noah all chose to trust God and obey Him. Through their obedience, they all pleased God. These three men remind us that even though we choose to follow God, the outcome of our lives may look wildly different.

Chapter 2: Isaac's Unforgettable Love Story

Focus: *What-ifs cause worry and stress. As children of God, we can walk in obedience and trust, knowing that God has all the details under control.*

1. What if the woman was unwilling to come back with him?

2. The servant prayed to God for a maiden who would not only give him a drink but also offer to draw water for his camels. Some participants may find they don't make specific requests to God for fear of those requests not being answered. Challenge the participants to pray for specific requests.

3. Answers will vary. Inward reflection will drive home the need for prayer over worry.

4. Answers will vary but could include

   What if I marry the wrong person?

   What if I don't get the job?

   What if I choose the wrong city to live in?

5. Emotionally, worrying always takes a toll on us by sapping our energy and evoking unhealthy responses. Spiritually, we have the opportunity to take each of these what-ifs to God and trust Him with all the details.

6. Encourage participants to continue to pray, especially when they feel overwhelmed with worries and what-if questions.

7. Isaac and Rebekah's meeting has evidence of the fingerprints of God. Rebekah was just the woman the servant was looking for and had prayed for. The Lord was fully in control of this situation.

8. Use the responses to these questions to enter a time of prayer as a group for the concerns mentioned.

Digging Deeper

Jesus prayed when He was faced with the ultimate what-if. He asked the Father if this cup could pass from Him. But in the end, He chose to follow His Father's will instead of His own. And aren't we glad He did? It was His obedience that provides our salvation. We can prepare for big what-if moments by choosing to trust God and walk in obedience in the little moments in life.

Chapter 3: Hagar Is Pursued by God

Focus: *Even when no one on earth understands the impossible situation you're facing, God sees you. That's a powerful encouragement not to worry but instead to trust in the God who sees.*

1. *When we listen to both sides of a story, we grow in compassion for both parties involved and are able to respond with more grace, love, wisdom, and compassion.*

2. *Some participants will completely relate to Hagar in her hopelessness. Encourage an honest time of sharing and discussion. If no one speaks up, consider sharing from your own life first.*

3. *She would have a son and too many descendants to count.*

4. *Often our plans don't exactly align with what God has planned for us.*

5. *Hagar was met by God both times. He saw her pain and offered hope. The first time, Hagar was in the desert place by her own choosing; the second time, she was forced there. Regardless of why she was there, the Lord offered hope and encouragement without condemnation.*

6. *Hagar's first trip to the desert and encounter with the Lord did not make her life trouble-free. Instead, Hagar finds herself later forced into the wilderness—this time with her child. But the Lord is faithful in His continued pursuit of Hagar.*

7. *Even though the Lord makes promises to us, that doesn't mean they will be fulfilled on our timetable. Often we need to wait patiently for the Lord to work in His own time. In Hagar's second encounter with the Lord, we see God's continued pursuit of Hagar, as He reiterates His initial promises to her. God is true to His word.*

8. *Answers*

Scripture	Promise
John 1:12	Example: Whoever believes in Jesus will not stay in darkness.
Proverbs 22:9	A generous man will be blessed.
Psalm 46:1	God is our refuge and our strength and will be present in our trouble.
Isaiah 43:1	The Lord has redeemed us and called us by name.
John 11:25	Jesus is the resurrection and the life. We receive eternal life through Him.
Isaiah 54:10	God's unfailing love for us will not be shaken.

While these passages only cover a small portion of the promises offered in Scripture, participants may resonate with one or more of them. Encourage the participants to find passages they love that offer a hopeful promise of the Lord.

Digging Deeper

Knowing God has a plan for her life should bring a great sense of peace to each participant. Knowing that the present situation is not the end will offer hope and encouragement in the middle of any seemingly impossible situation. Hagar surely would have been encouraged by such a verse; after all, it is nearly the same promise she received from the angel.

Chapter 4: Sarah's Echoing Laughter

Focus: *Even when it seems all hope is gone, we can still choose to trust God. Nothing is too hard for the Lord.*

1. *Abraham ran to the men, bowed before them, and was hospitable toward them. Sarah was tired and worn out. And she laughed. What the Lord said seemed 100% impossible in her eyes. In Sarah's shoes, we all may have been tempted to laugh at the news.*

2. *Like Sarah, we are all tempted to laugh at the seeming impossibility of some situations. Often those who have trust and faith in the situation may take our laughter as rude or inconsiderate. Other times, people may laugh along with us.*

3. *God asks, "Is anything too hard for the Lord?" Sometimes we all need to be reminded that nothing is too hard for the Lord. This question is designed to help participants personalize the power of the Lord in their own circumstances.*

4. *Sarah (Sarai, before the Lord changes her name) didn't trust the Lord to fulfill His promise and give her a son, so she had her servant sleep with her husband. Hagar and Abraham had a child named Ishmael—whom God promised would also become a father to many nations. Sarah became jealous of the woman and her son and treated her harshly.*

5. As humans, we often desire to take matters into our own hands rather than trust God. Usually our plans fail miserably.

6. The Lord kept his promise to her and gave her a son at the very time he had promised he would. Sarah remarked on her laughter and stated that everyone who heard this story would laugh also because no one thought she would be able to have a child.

7. Encourage participants to reflect on any answered prayers or situations where God has proved himself faithful.

8. Answers will vary.

Digging Deeper

Zechariah was frightened when confronted by the angel. He didn't believe what the angel said to him because he was so old. Elizabeth was excited and no longer felt ashamed of her barrenness when she found out she was pregnant. Mary was startled by what the angel said to her but was obedient. These three unexpected parents were startled by the news of their children-to-be, but each trusted that nothing is impossible with God.

Chapter 5: Joseph's Unexpected Rise to Power

Focus: God can be trusted with all your dreams—big or small. He has a plan and a purpose for your life. Even when the stresses of everyday life come, He is there working behind the scenes on your behalf.

1. Jacob made Joseph a special coat of many colors—he treated him as his favorite.

2. Encourage the participants to engage in conversation with one another regarding parental favoritism and its effects.

3. All the sheaves of his brothers gathered around and bowed down to his sheaf, and the sun, moon, and eleven stars all bowed down to Joseph as well. In both dreams, Joseph was elevated above his brothers, and this provoked their already jealous hearts to take cruel action.

4. Joseph refused to be alone with Potiphar's wife and did not fall into temptation. In both good times and bad, Joseph recognized the hand of the Lord upon him. He would not bring dishonor to his God. It is common for everyone to go through some sort of temptation, but Joseph stayed faithful despite temptation and suffered unfair consequences.

5. Answers

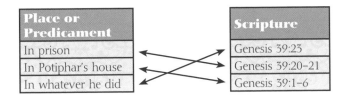

Place or Predicament	Scripture
In prison	Genesis 39:23
In Potiphar's house	Genesis 39:20–21
In whatever he did	Genesis 39:1–6

God is always with us, whether we notice it or not.

6. Answers

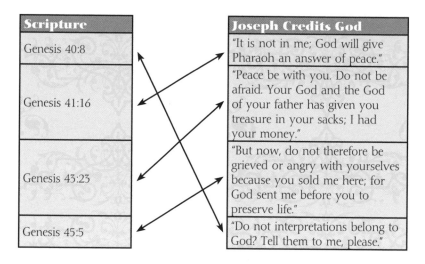

Scripture	Joseph Credits God
Genesis 40:8	"It is not in me; God will give Pharaoh an answer of peace."
Genesis 41:16	"Peace be with you. Do not be afraid. Your God and the God of your father has given you treasure in your sacks; I had your money."
Genesis 43:23	"But now, do not therefore be grieved or angry with yourselves because you sold me here; for God sent me before you to preserve life."
Genesis 45:5	"Do not interpretations belong to God? Tell them to me, please."

God. This same powerful God who granted favor to Joseph is able to make our dreams come true today. It may be easy for us to want to take the credit for God's actions, but in reality, the Lord blesses us with every talent and ability we have. To Him be the all of the glory.

7. God uses all kinds of unusual circumstances to lead us and guide us in our families, workplaces, and daily lives.

8. Encourage participants to be bold in trusting the Lord with their dreams.

Digging Deeper

Answers will vary. God is so much bigger than we can even imagine. He will do much more than we can ever dream. Trust in Him fully with your relationships, jobs, families, and lives.

Chapter 6: Esther's Divine Moment

Focus: *We don't have to worry because God is at work even when we don't recognize it. We can trust God with everything.*

1. Answers

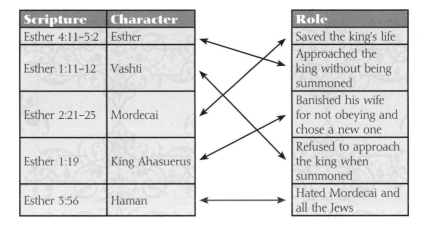

Scripture	Character		Role
Esther 4:11–5:2	Esther		Saved the king's life
Esther 1:11–12	Vashti		Approached the king without being summoned
Esther 2:21–23	Mordecai		Banished his wife for not obeying and chose a new one
Esther 1:19	King Ahasuerus		Refused to approach the king when summoned
Esther 3:56	Haman		Hated Mordecai and all the Jews

This question is designed to engage participants in a fun discussion about their favorite Bible characters.

2. The Jews would all die if she failed. While we may not be faced with the fate of an entire race of people, there are often situations where we feel the weight and pressure of needing to succeed.

3. She would have been executed immediately unless he chose to hold out the royal gold scepter in mercy.

4. *Answers will vary. When God asks something big of us, we may not want to take the risk. We may be more willing to do the small things, but risking our lives as Esther did is a big commitment to make.*

5. *Participants will have various examples of times where they were distinctly and uniquely chosen for a particular job. Celebrate the times where God chose to use each person "for such a time as this."*

6. *Esther had the courage to stand up and confront the king and Haman about the plot against the Jews. The timing is also important, as Haman had planned to kill Mordecai.*

7. *Answers will vary. Esther's boldness and willingness to stand up for her people can be seen as courage from the Lord. God obviously wanted to save His people, so He prepared the way for Esther and Mordecai to work on His behalf. There are many times in our own stories where we may not hear the Lord's voice or see His presence, but we know He is working in us and around us.*

8. *Answers will vary.*

Digging Deeper

Even though Esther's parents were not in the picture, God used her uncle to take care of her. Even though she was snatched from her home, she became queen and was uniquely in the position to risk talking to the king on behalf of the Jewish people. Whatever happens in life, God is always able to redeem any situation for His glory if we walk in faith and obedience.

Chapter 7: Moses Protests His Divine Calling

Focus: *At times you may feel inadequate to do the very things God has created and called you to do, but you can find confidence knowing that the God who has chosen you will be with you every step of the way.*

1. *1, 4, 7, 3, 6, 2, 5*

2. *This question is designed to initiate a conversation about inadequacy. When we worry and doubt ourselves instead of trusting in the Lord, we are limiting what God can do through us. Encourage the participants to go to the Lord with any inadequacies they feel.*

3. *Moses answered, "Here I am." That is the response we should always have when we hear the voice of God in our hearts. It is often easy for us to ignore God calling us as we don't all have burning bush-like encounters with the Lord.*

4. *Answers*

Scripture	Moses's Concern	God's Response
Exodus 3:11–12	Who am I that I should go?	The Lord would go with Moses.
Exodus 3:13–14	What if they ask me, "What is His name?"	"I Am."
Exodus 4:1–9	What if they do not believe me?	He gave Moses signs to prove to the Egyptians.
Exodus 4:10–12	O Lord, I have never been eloquent.	The Lord reminded Moses who gave him his mouth and who is in charge. He would teach Moses what to say.
Exodus 4:13–16	Please send someone else to do it.	The Lord sent Aaron with Moses.

5. *Answers will vary, but excuses and reasons can include a lack of experience, being unqualified, feeling untalented, lack of time, lack of skill, age, background, education, and many more.*

6. *Answers will vary, but when God asks us to do something, He's already convinced we're the perfect choice.*

7. *Share something from your own life first to encourage others to open up about their journeys.*

8. *Encourage participants to share from their own experiences, and close in a time of prayer.*

Digging Deeper

The passage notes that Moses refused to be known as the son of Pharaoh's daughter, thus siding more with the Hebrew people than with the Egyptians. Moses repeatedly made this choice, even choosing to leave Egypt and fulfill the calling God had for his life.

Chapter 8: David Dances with Wild Abandon

Focus: *When we choose to worship rather than worry, all our anxiety and concerns melt away in the presence of God. Worship is always the better choice.*

1. *Encourage everyone's different responses as worship takes so many different forms.*

2. Answers

_X_ Rejoicing

___ Waving a banner

_X_ Blessing others in
    the name of the
    Lord

_X_ Listening to
    trumpets blasting

___ Singing "In Christ
    Alone"

_X_ Leaping

___ Holding hands
    with his wife

_X_ Sacrificing burnt
    offerings

_X_ Dancing before
    the Lord

_X_ Shouting

_X_ Celebrating before
    the Lord

___ Playing his harp

3. Answers will vary, but often the responses that are easiest and most natural for us are those that are the most familiar. Sometimes we choose not to express worship to God in a particular way simply because it is foreign or new to us.

4. Answers will vary. This question is designed to help participants recall a true worship experience if they have had one, and if not, then subtly to bring that to their attention as well.

5. Answers will vary. She may have been angered by her husband's absence or his behavior, which was not very dignified for a king. What was pleasing in God's eyes was embarrassing to Michal.

6. Answers will vary.

7. *Michal's life is more heartbreak than hope. Not only did she miss out on celebrating with her husband, David, but she also despised him and his response to the work God was doing not only in his life but also throughout the entire kingdom. This was an amazing day of celebration, and Michal missed it.*

8. *Worship often requires us to be intentional and to focus ourselves–our whole selves–on God. We can prompt a more worshipful response to God by using a variety of expressions including music, dance, silence, artwork, singing, and simply being with Him.*

Digging Deeper

Answers will vary. According to verse 7, God isn't focused on the way a person looks or what people think about them. God is concerned with the heart. When we remember that, we are more able to live a life free from fear of condemnation or judgment.

Chapter 9: Cain's Reminder About What's Truly Important

Focus: *When swirling emotions threaten to take over, we have a choice. Let's choose to obey God, surrender all our anxiety, and let peace reign in our hearts and lives.*

1. *Answers will vary.*

Anger	*Overwhelmed*
Regret	*Rage*
Jealousy	*Shame*
Discouragement	*Fear*
Pride	*Frustration*

2. Answers will vary, but often we find ourselves directing our negative emotions toward ourselves, God, and those who are closest to us in proximity and relationship.

3. Encourage participants to share openly and honestly. If no one wants to share, have something prepared as a leader to share, and set the level of intimacy for the group.

4. Answers will vary. This question is designed to motivate participants to think about the true stress relievers that make a real difference, including spending time with the Lord.

5. Encourage participants to share from specific moments of work, school, or everyday life.

6. Encourage participants to share from specific moments of work, school, or everyday life.

7. Answers

Paul Instructs Believers to Focus On	How My Life Demonstrates That Focus
Example: True	Answers will vary.
Noble	
Right	
Pure	
Lovely	
Admirable	
Excellent	
Praiseworthy	

8. *Give participants some time and space to engage in this activity and reflect on the question themselves. You may want to play soft music in the background if it's easily available. You may want to read Matthew 5:44–45 during this time.*

Digging Deeper

The Scriptures remind us that God stills the raging storms not just on the sea but also in our lives and hearts.

Chapter 10: Abraham's Big Decision

Focus: *Worrying about past mistakes only robs us of future progress. God will still forgive, teach, and use us for His glory. Even when we fail Him, He never fails us.*

1. *The same God who walked alongside Abraham despite his deception and lack of faith is the one we serve today.*

2. *Answers will vary. Encourage participants to share times when they are tempted to trust themselves over God.*

3. *The Lord inflicted serious diseases on Pharaoh and his household.*

4. *The Lord confronted Abimelech in a dream and told him that Sarah was married. Even when we make mistakes, the will of the Lord will be done.*

5. *Answers will vary.*

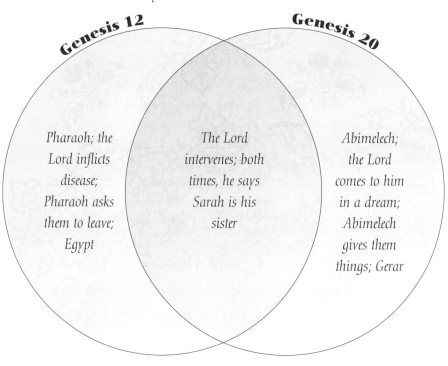

Genesis 12

Genesis 20

Pharaoh; the Lord inflicts disease; Pharaoh asks them to leave; Egypt

The Lord intervenes; both times, he says Sarah is his sister

Abimelech; the Lord comes to him in a dream; Abimelech gives them things; Gerar

6. *Answers will vary.*

7. *Answers will vary. Gently encourage participants to share their responses. Lead your group in prayer asking for freedom and forgiveness from our past selves so we can fully enter a life of forgiveness through the grace of God.*

8. *The Lord is sure to forgive us for any past mistake, just as He forgave Abraham. He still chooses to use us for His plan and purpose. Encourage participants to spend time in prayer and in the Word.*

Digging Deeper

Abraham's belief in the Lord is credited as righteousness. "For the promise that he would be the heir of the world was not to Abraham or to his seed through the law, but through the righteousness of faith." Paul does not emphasize a works-based salvation, but instead a faith-based one. It is not because of what we do that we are considered righteous; it is instead by our belief and faith in the Lord. Despite Abraham's past, he was still considered faithful and was still known for his great faith.

Chapter 11: Ruth's Amazing Rescue

Focus: *Though we are faced with seasons of loss and pain, God has a plan not only to provide for us but also heal us. We simply need to turn and trust him.*

1. Ruth and Naomi are very close, more like mother and daughter than mother-in-law and daughter-in-law. Ruth is loyal to Naomi and pledges to go wherever she goes.

2. Encourage participants to share from their own lives. Whether because of financial, physical, or relational struggles, most people have found themselves in need of help from others. In those times, we often learn of our true need for other people and the gracious provision of God, among other lessons.

3. Whether donating food to a local food bank, volunteering hours at a women's shelter or soup kitchen, or sharing the extras of your meals with neighbors, there are countless ways we can practice sharing the corners of our fields with others.

4. Leviticus 25:23–28 says that relatives are required to redeem their relatives in need. Deuteronomy 25:5–6 gives instructions on how families are to take care of widows.

5. Boaz and Ruth's great-grandson is David, a man who became one of Israel's greatest leaders. The lineage of David leads directly to the birth of Jesus Christ. Thus, Ruth and Boaz became the ancestors of Jesus, who was born in Bethlehem. A woman whose life was marked by pain and loss became an ancestor of the Son of God, the one who gave His life for the world.

6. Guide women to share their answers to this question, and be prepared with reassuring words for them. Don't minimize the emotion they might be feeling about the situations they describe, but do point them to God's Word and encourage them to continue trusting God's faithfulness and power.

7. Encourage participants to share honestly. Encourage participants to celebrate the God wins in their lives, the ways they tangibly see God moving, working, providing, and answering prayer. No God sighting is too small to celebrate.

8. Give participants some time and space to reflect on this question; then, engage in prayer as a group for the needs mentioned. At the next gathering, remember to ask for any praise reports of answered prayers from participants.

Digging Deeper

Jesus sacrificed His own life in order to become our kinsman redeemer, the One who saved us. Just as Boaz redeemed Ruth, giving her a life and a future, so too does Jesus want to redeem us from our sins—an act of redemption we could never do for ourselves—and give us a life and a future with Him.

Chapter 12: Elijah's Divine Visitation

Focus: *Even when we are emotionally, spiritually, and physically overwhelmed by stress and worry, God longs to speak to our souls in a gentle whisper and assure us of His presence and purpose for our lives.*

1. *Because Elijah killed the prophets of Baal (1 Kings 18:40), Jezebel made an oath to kill Elijah within twenty-four hours. Terrified, Elijah ran for his life.*

2. *Encourage participants to consider situations where they have run away from their relationships or commitments because they became too difficult.*

3. *Answers should vary greatly. The order of the worries isn't as important as the idea that Elijah had a lot to worry about.*

4. *Answers should vary greatly. The order of the worries isn't as important as the idea that Elijah had a lot to worry about.*

5. *Encourage participants to share honestly.*

6. *Encourage participants to share honestly.*

7. Answers

Scripture	Elijah's Worry	God's Response
1 Kings 19:16	Elijah was worried that Jezebel and Ahab would continue to rule the land.	Jehu would be king and Elisha would succeed Elijah.
1 Kings 19:5–6	Elijah was worried that he would not have food to eat or water to drink in the desert.	The Lord provided food and water.
1 Kings 19:18	Elijah was worried that he was the only one who still faithfully followed God.	Seven thousand faithful remained.
1 Kings 19:11	Elijah was worried that God didn't notice or care for him.	The Lord showed Elijah His presence.
1 Kings 19:15	Elijah was worried that his life and ministry were over forever.	The Lord gave him further instructions.

8. Answers will vary. The Lord will never leave our side and is faithful despite our worry and stress.

Digging Deeper

Elisha chose to go back and say goodbye to his family. He wanted to get his affairs in order. However, Jesus desires wholehearted commitment. Often, we are tempted to make sure our lives are in perfect condition before obeying the Lord.

About the Author

A popular speaker at churches and leading conferences such as Catalyst and Thrive, Margaret Feinberg was recently named one of the "30 Voices" who will help lead the church in the next decade by *Charisma* magazine. She has written more than two dozen books and Bible studies, including the critically acclaimed *The Organic God*, *The Sacred Echo*, *Scouting the Divine*, and their corresponding DVD Bible studies. She is known for her relational teaching style and inviting people to discover the relevance of God and His Word in a modern world.

Margaret and her books have been covered by national media, including: CNN, the Associated Press, *Los Angeles Times*, Dallas Morning News, *Washington Post*, *Chicago Tribune*, and many others. She currently lives in Colorado, with her 6'8" husband, Leif, and superpup, Hershey. Go ahead, become her friend on Facebook, follow her on Twitter @mafeinberg, add her on Google+ or check out her website at www.margaretfeinberg.com.